FOR ORGANS, PIANOS & ELECTRONIC KEYBOARDS

E-Z PLAY TODAY®

305

ROD STEWART
BEST OF THE GREAT AMERICAN SONGBOOK

Cover photo: Paul Cox / LFI

ISBN 978-1-4234-8757-9

HAL•LEONARD®
CORPORATION

7777 W. BLUEMOUND RD. P.O. BOX 13819 MILWAUKEE, WI 53213

E-Z Play® Today Music Notation © 1975 by HAL LEONARD CORPORATION
E-Z PLAY and EASY ELECTRONIC KEYBOARD MUSIC are registered trademarks of HAL LEONARD CORPORATION.

Visit Hal Leonard Online at
www.halleonard.com

Baby, It's Cold Outside
from the Motion Picture NEPTUNE'S DAUGHTER

Registration 1
Rhythm: Fox Trot

By Frank Loesser

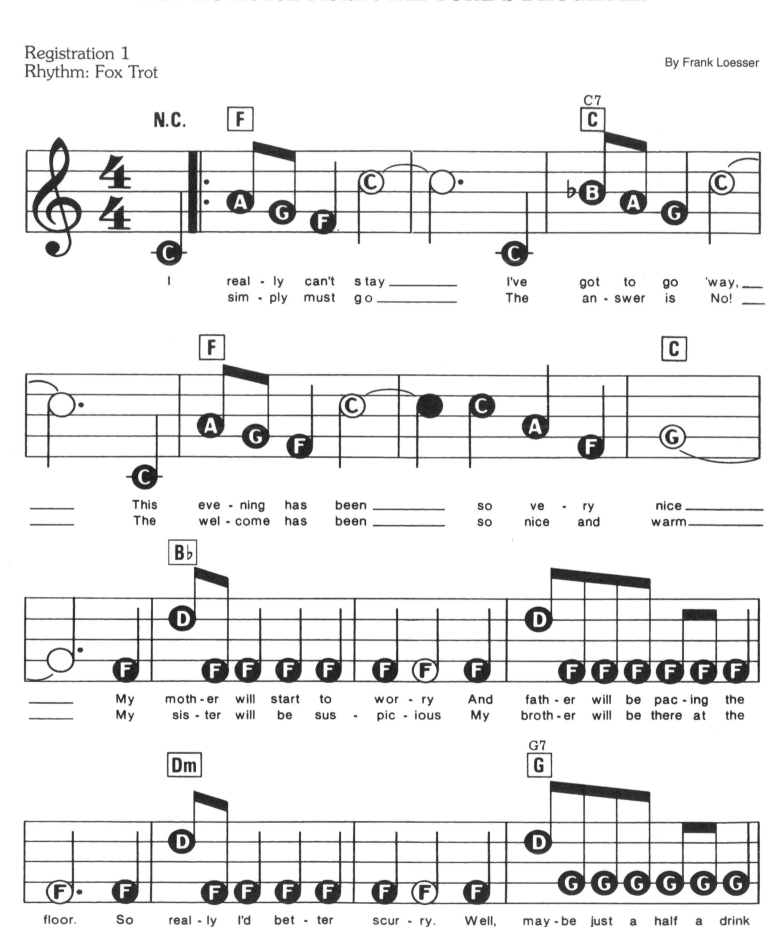

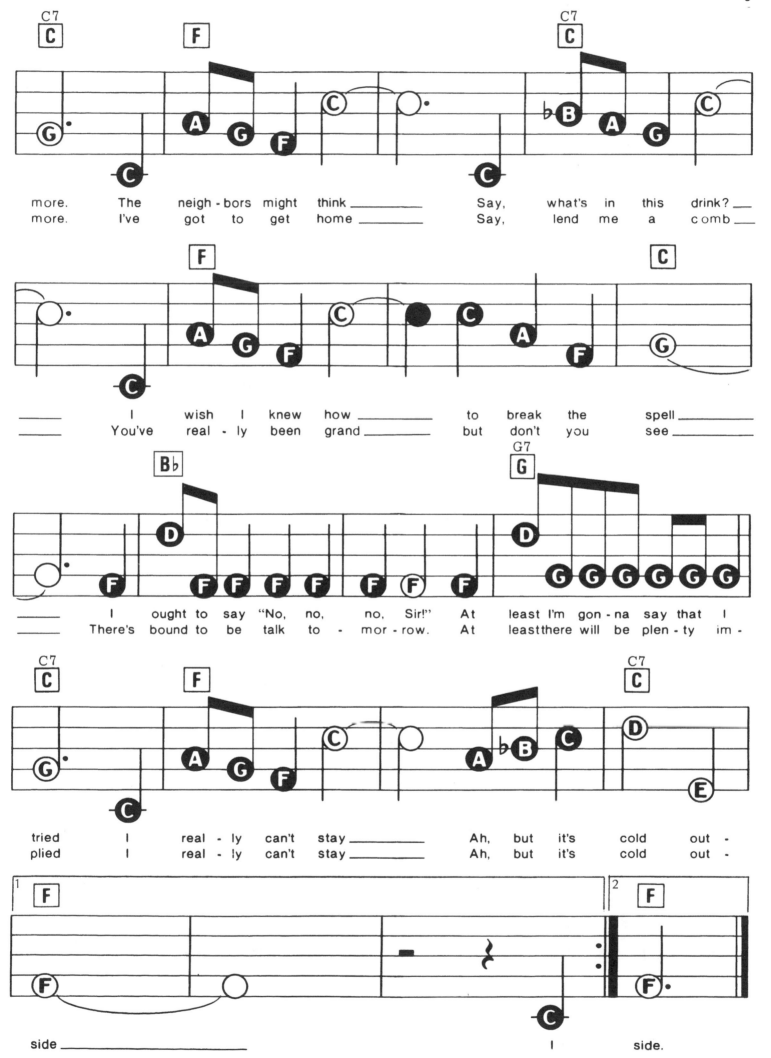

more. The neigh-bors might think _____ Say, what's in this drink? ___
more. I've got to get home _____ Say, lend me a comb ___

_____ I wish I knew how _____ to break the spell _____
_____ You've real-ly been grand _____ but don't you see _____

_____ I ought to say "No, no, no, Sir!" At least I'm gon-na say that I
_____ There's bound to be talk to-mor-row. At leastthere will be plen-ty im-

tried I real-ly can't stay _____ Ah, but it's cold out -
plied I real-ly can't stay _____ Ah, but it's cold out -

side _____ side.

Crazy She Calls Me

Registration 1
Rhythm: Fox Trot or Ballad

Music by Carl Sigman
Lyrics by Bob Russell

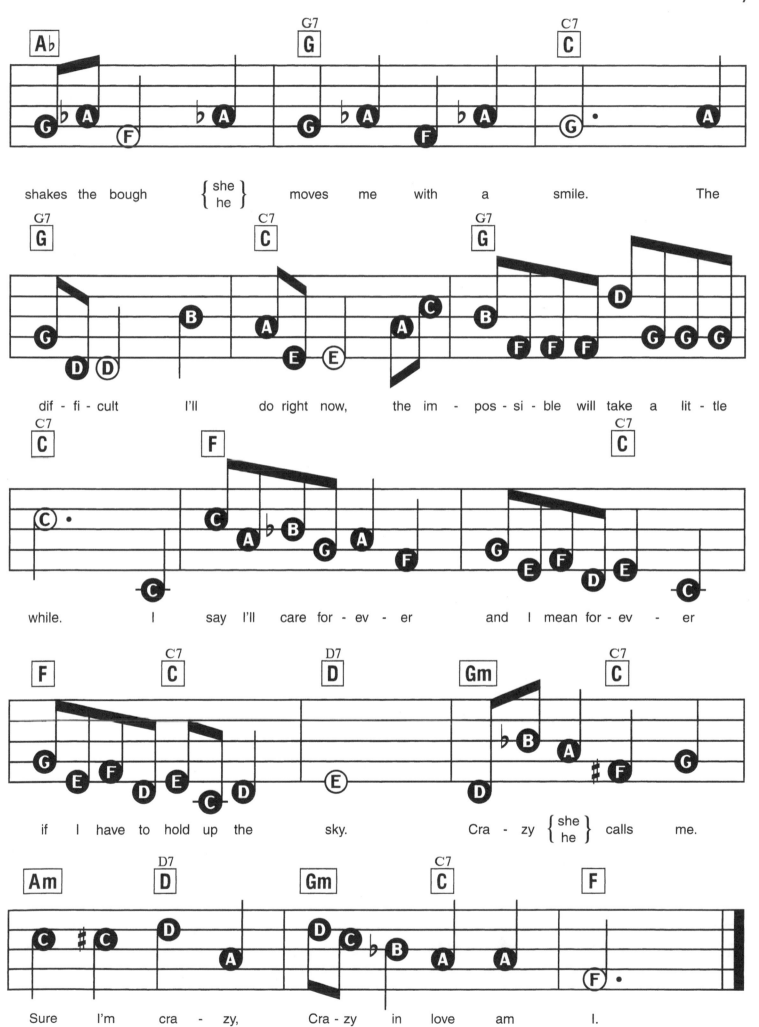

Don't Get Around Much Anymore
from SOPHISTICATED LADY

Registration 7
Rhythm: Swing

Words and Music by Duke Ellington
and Bob Russell

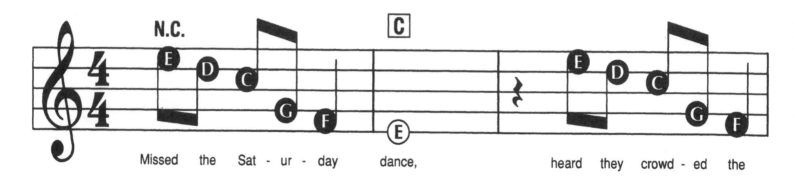

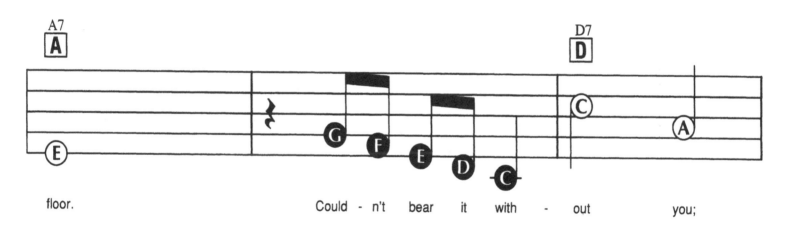

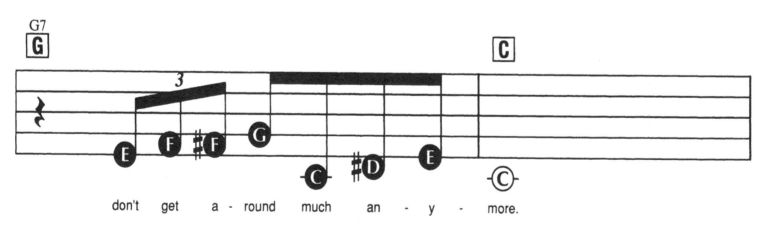

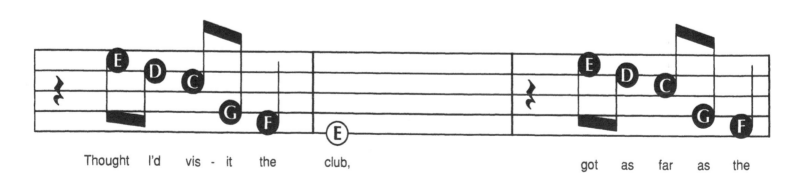

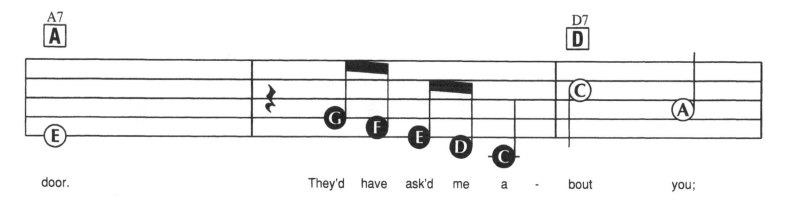

door. They'd have ask'd me a - bout you;

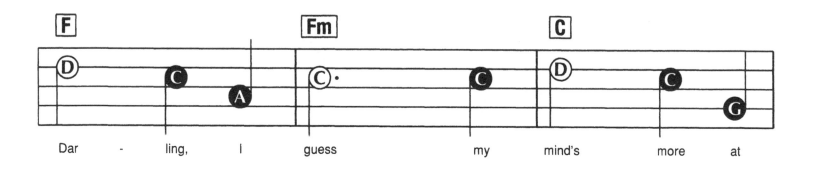

don't get a - round much an - y - more. _____

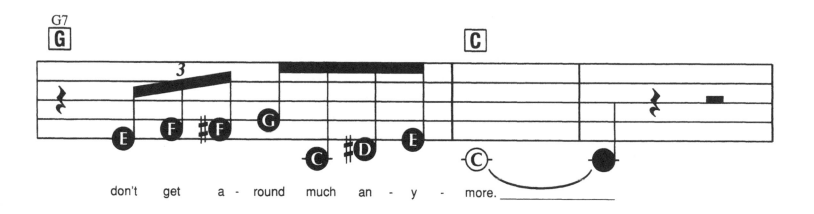

Dar - ling, I guess my mind's more at

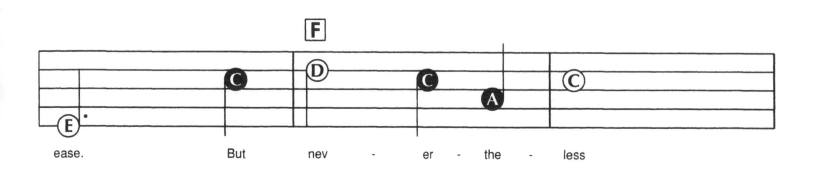

ease. But nev - er - the - less

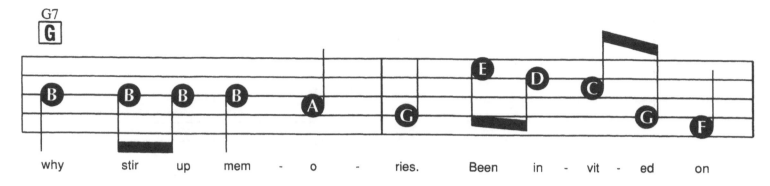

why stir up mem - o - ries. Been in - vit - ed on

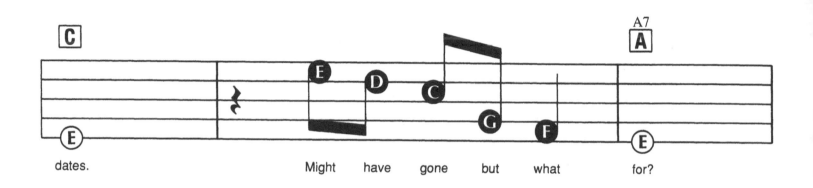

dates. Might have gone but what for?

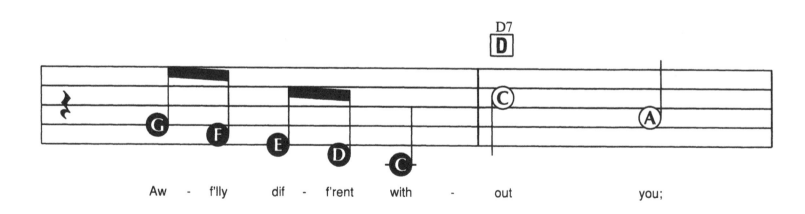

Aw - f'lly dif - f'rent with - out you;

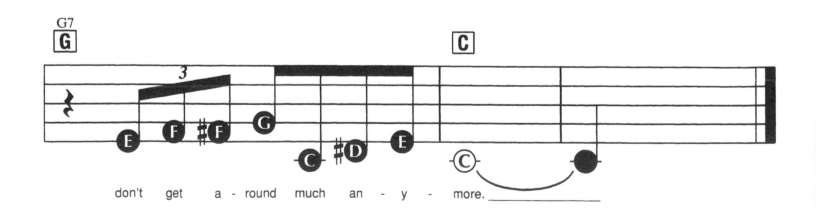

don't get a - round much an - y - more. _____

Ev'ry Time We Say Goodbye
from SEVEN LIVELY ARTS

Registration 1
Rhythm: Latin or Bossa Nova

Words and Music by
Cole Porter

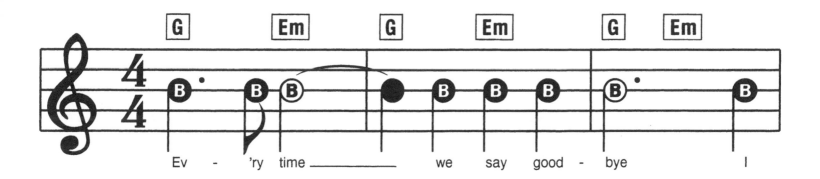

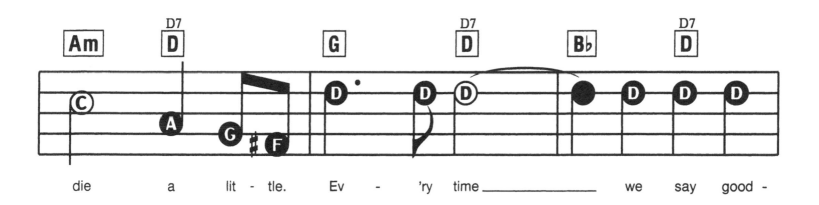

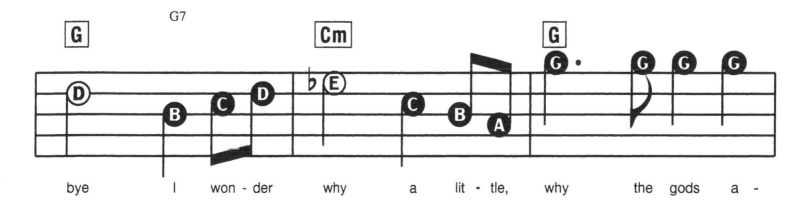

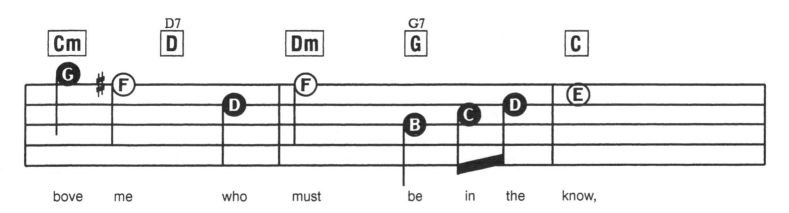

12

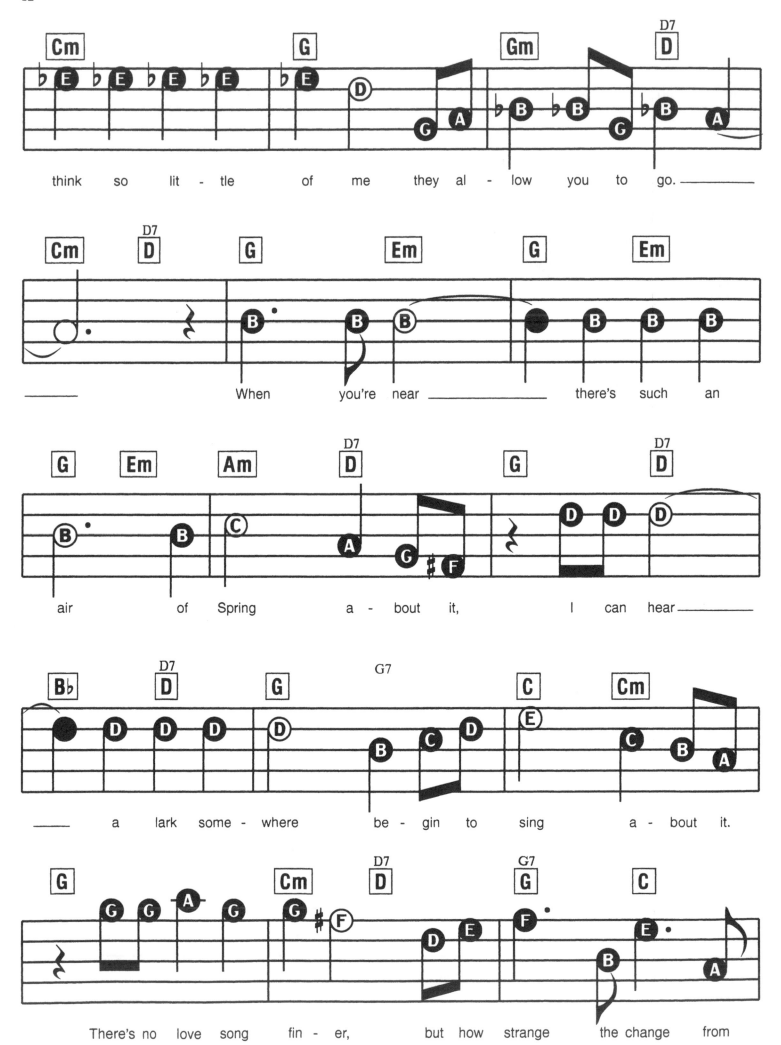

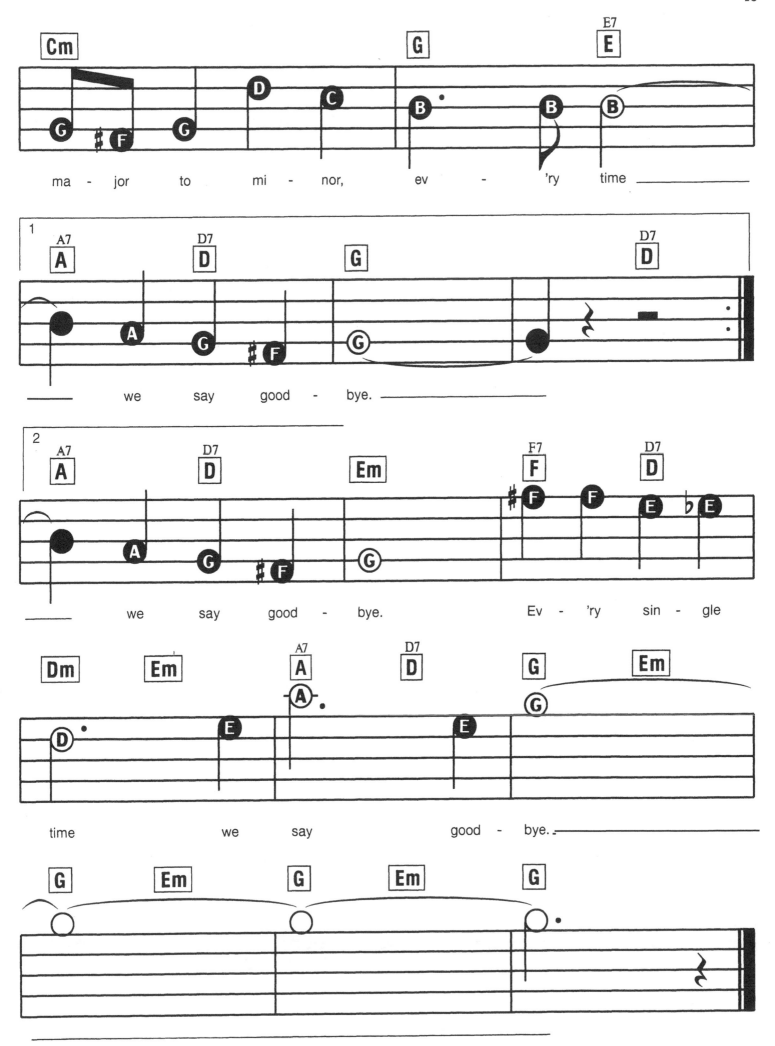

For All We Know

Registration 1
Rhythm: Swing

Words by Sam M. Lewis
Music by J. Fred Coots

N.C. | **F** | **G**

For all we know we may

C7
C

nev - er meet a - gain, Be - fore you

D7
D | **Gm** | **B♭m**

go make this mo - ment sweet a - gain, We

F | **Dm** | **Gm**

won't say good - night un - til the last

C7
C | **F** | **Dm**

min - ute, I'll hold out my hand and my

I Wish You Love

Registration 8
Rhythm: Latin

English Words by Albert Beach
French Words and Music by Charles Trenet

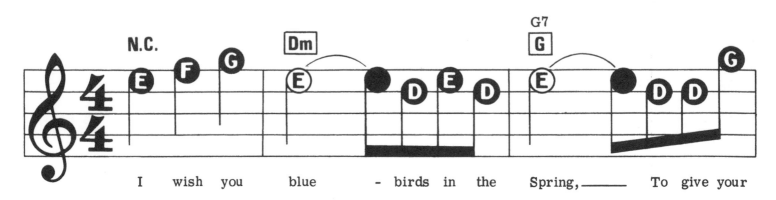

I wish you blue - birds in the Spring, _____ To give your

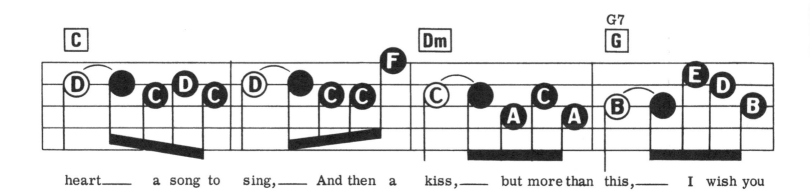

heart____ a song to sing,____ And then a kiss,____ but more than this,____ I wish you

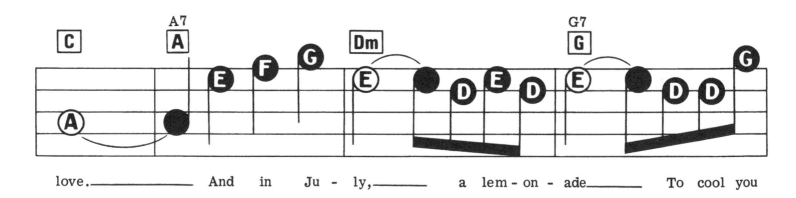

love.____ And in Ju - ly,____ a lem - on - ade____ To cool you

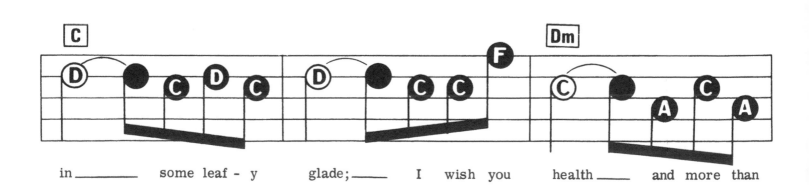

in____ some leaf - y glade;____ I wish you health____ and more than

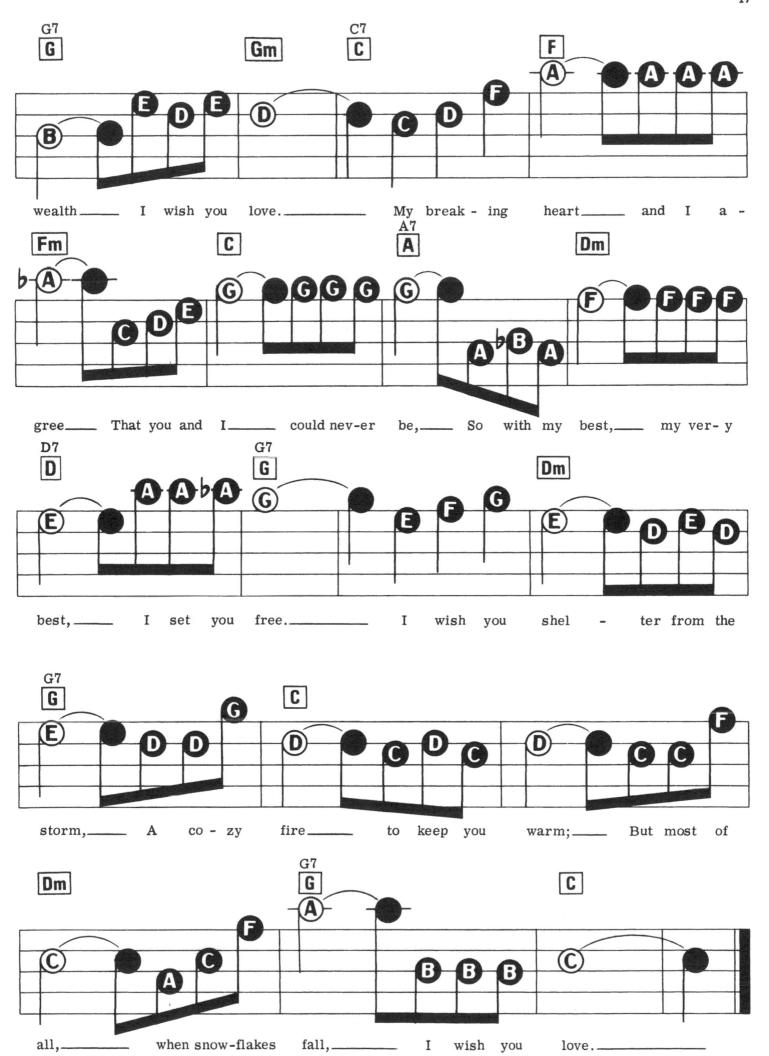

I'll Be Seeing You

from RIGHT THIS WAY

Registration 5
Rhythm: Ballad or Swing

Written by Irving Kahal
and Sammy Fain

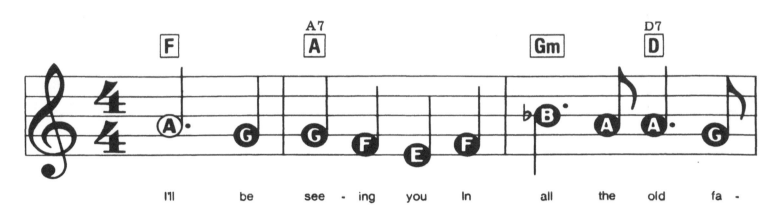

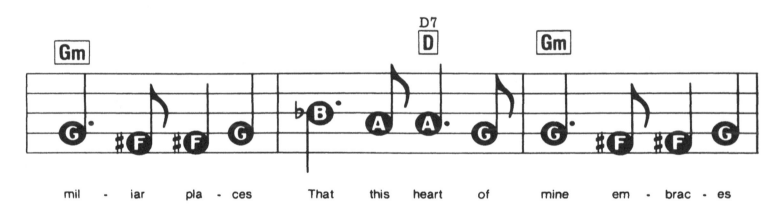

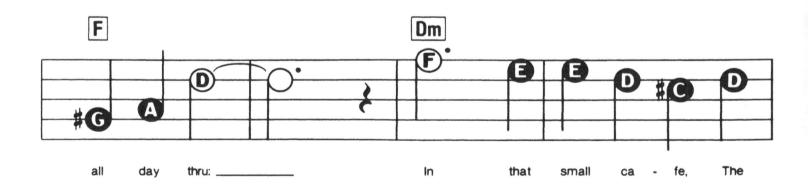

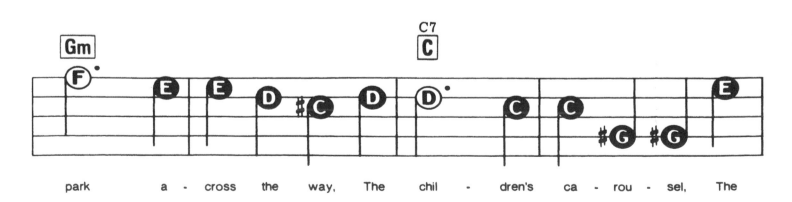

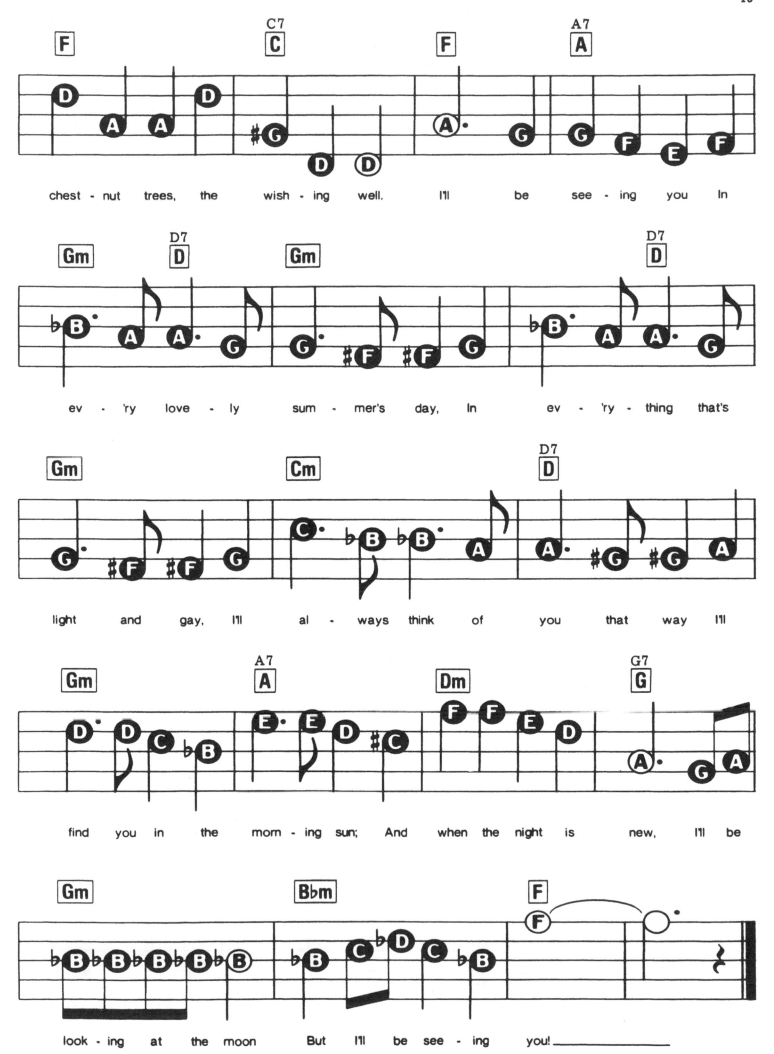

It Will Have to Do Until the Real Thing Comes Along

Registration 8
Rhythm: Fox Trot or Ballad

Words and Music by Mann Holiner,
Alberta Nichols, Saul Chaplin,
L.E. Freeman and Sammy Cahn

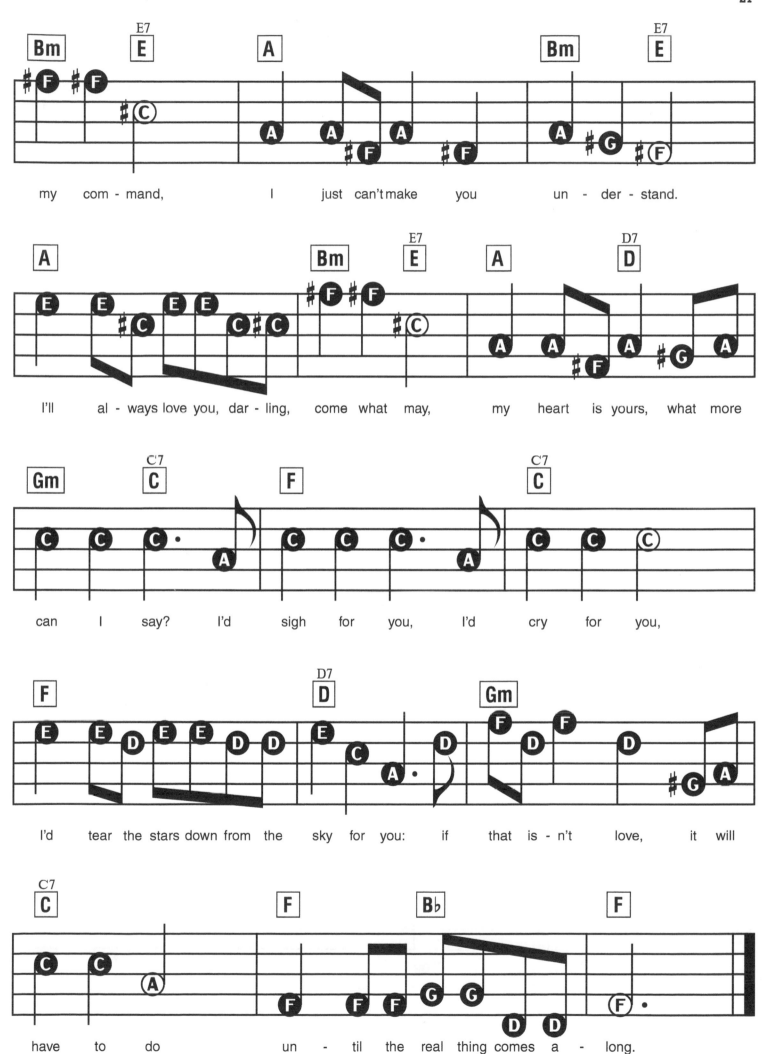

Moonglow

Registration 2
Rhythm: Fox Trot

Words and Music by Will Hudson,
Eddie De Lange and Irving Mills

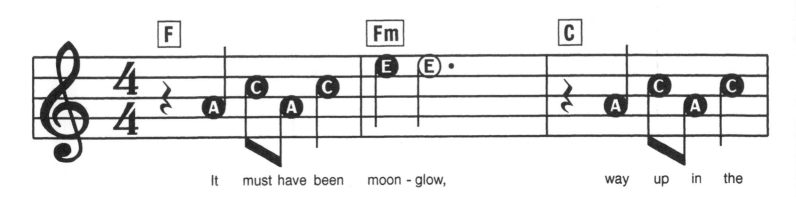

It must have been moon - glow, way up in the

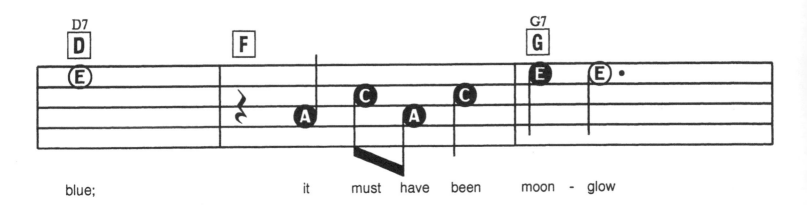

blue; it must have been moon - glow

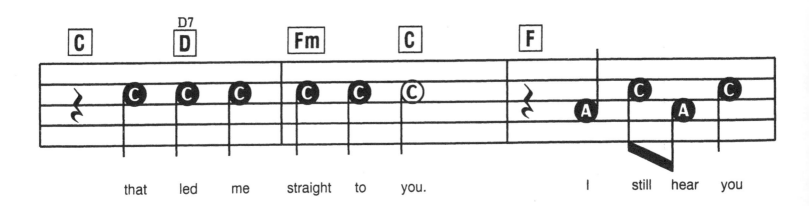

that led me straight to you. I still hear you

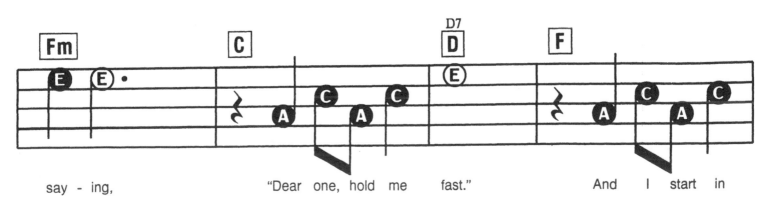

say - ing, "Dear one, hold me fast." And I start in

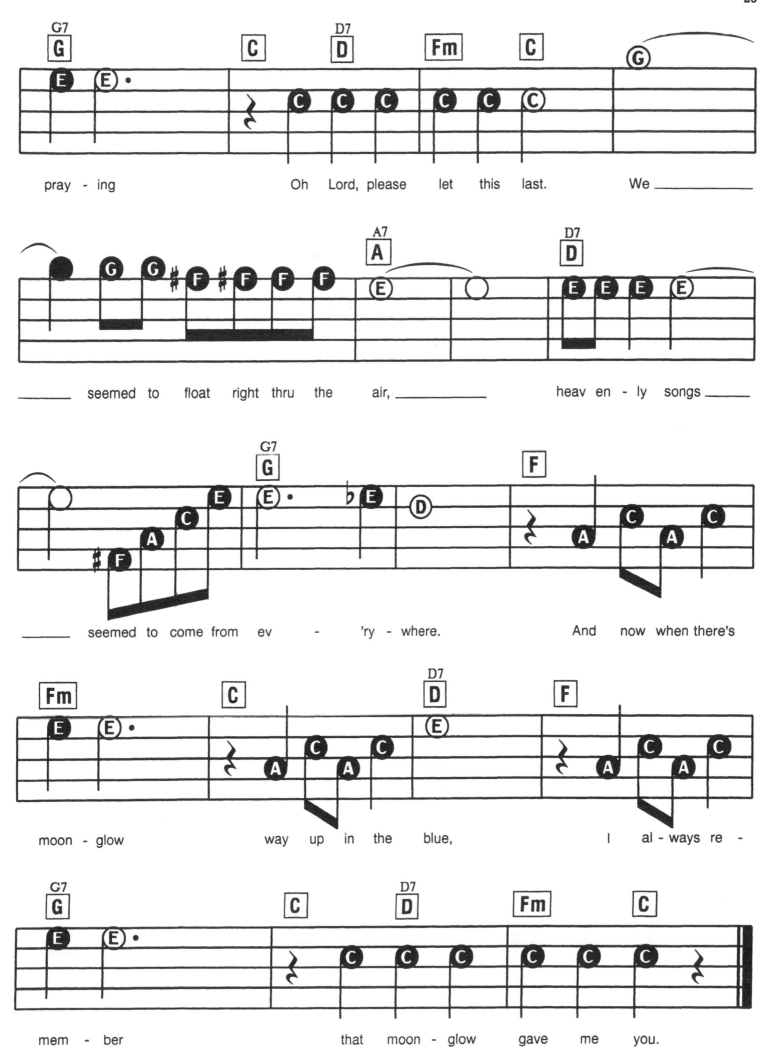

My Heart Stood Still
from A CONNECTICUT YANKEE

Registration 4
Rhythm: Swing

Words by Lorenz Hart
Music by Richard Rodgers

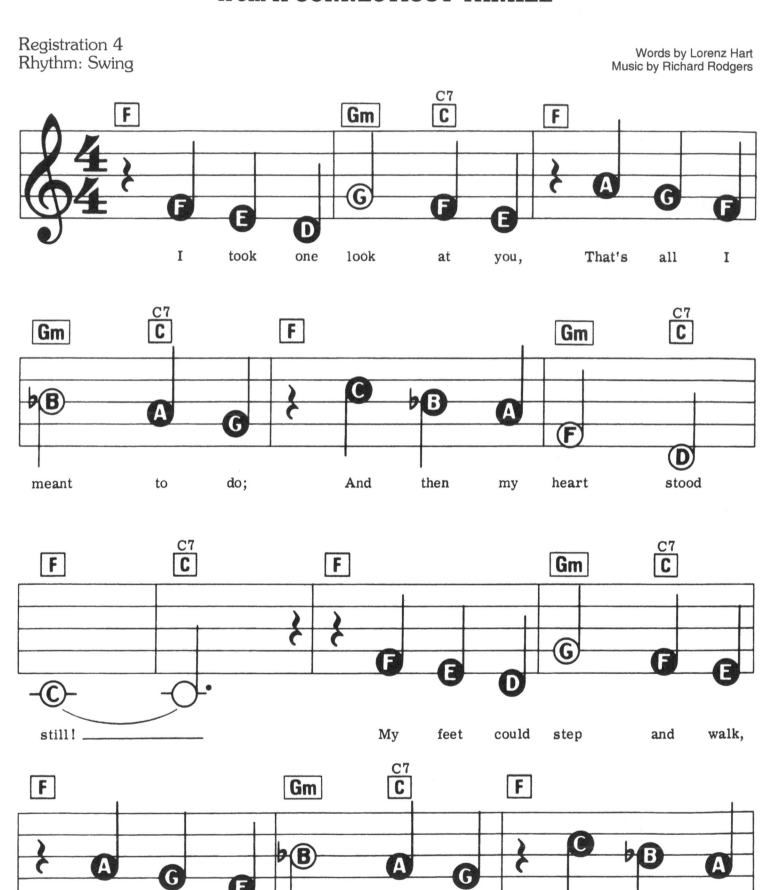

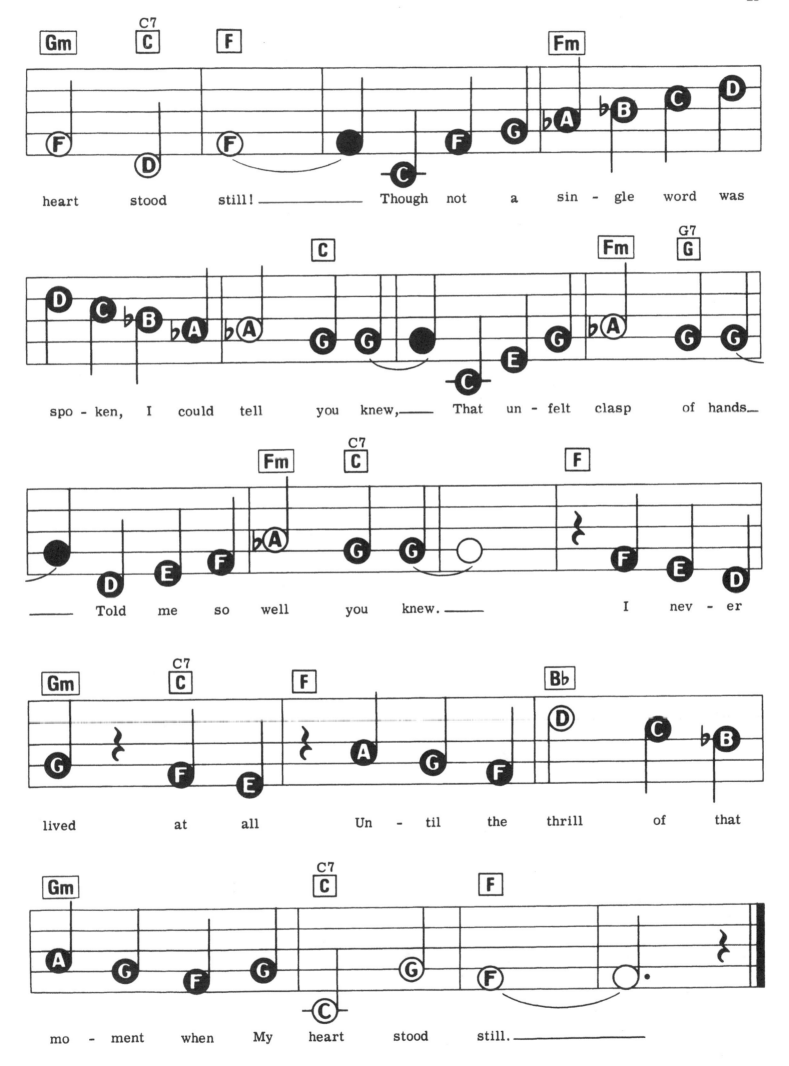

The Nearness of You
from the Paramount Picture ROMANCE IN THE DARK

Registration 9
Rhythm: Ballad or Fox Trot

Words by Ned Washington
Music by Hoagy Carmichael

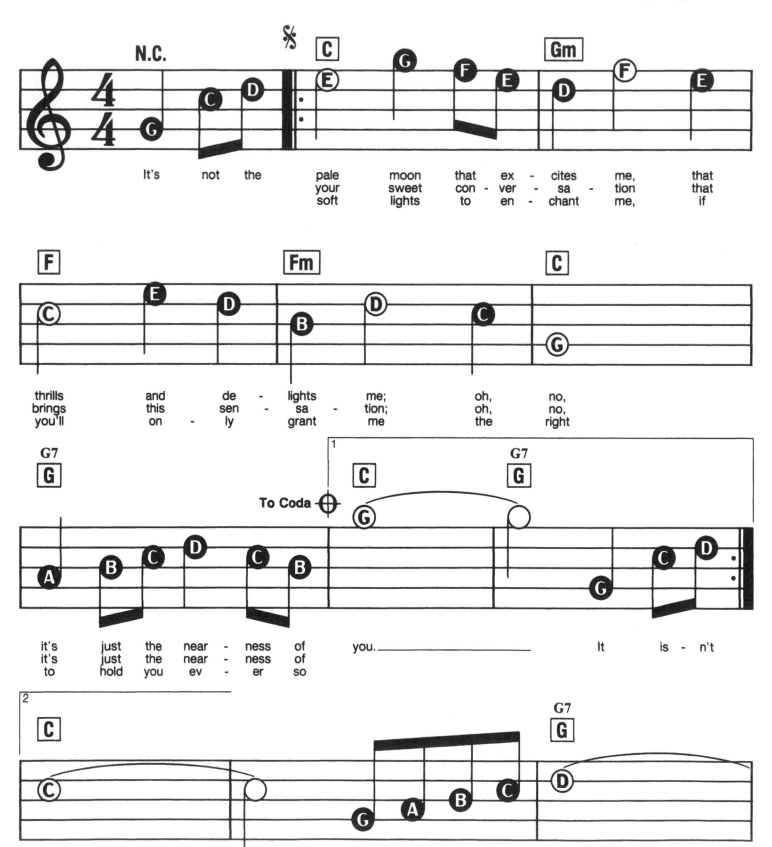

It's not the pale moon that ex - cites me, that
your sweet con - ver - sa - tion that
soft lights to en - chant me, if

thrills and de - lights me; oh, no,
brings this sen - sa - tion; oh, no,
you'll on - ly grant me the right

it's just the near - ness of you._____ It is - n't
it's just the near - ness of you._____
to hold you ev - er so

you._____ When you're in my arms_____

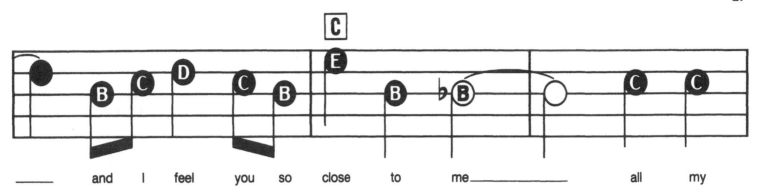

and I feel you so close to me_____ all my

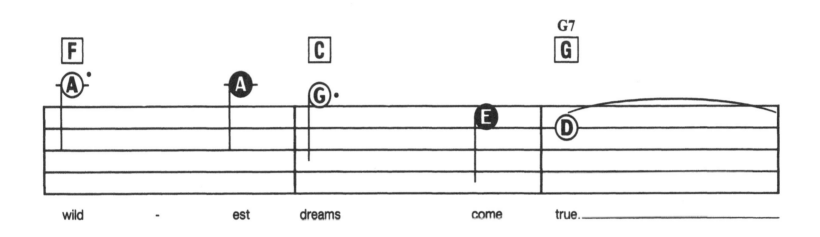

wild - est dreams come true._____

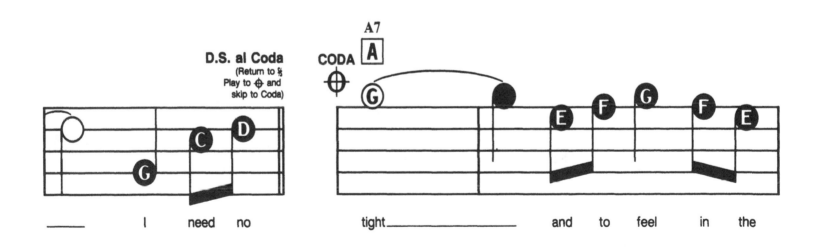

_____ I need no

tight_____ and to feel in the

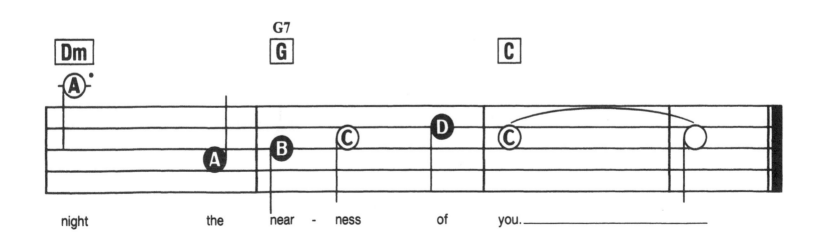

night the near - ness of you._____

Smile
Theme from MODERN TIMES

Registration 9
Rhythm: Ballad or Fox Trot

Words by John Turner and Geoffrey Parsons
Music by Charles Chaplin

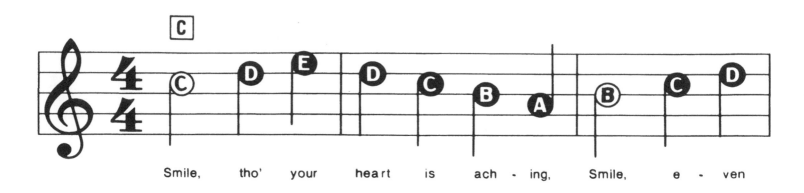

Smile, tho' your heart is ach - ing, Smile, e - ven

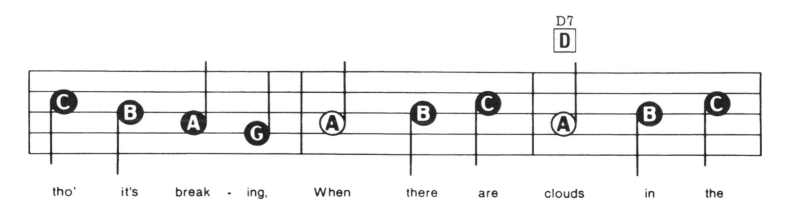

tho' it's break - ing, When there are clouds in the

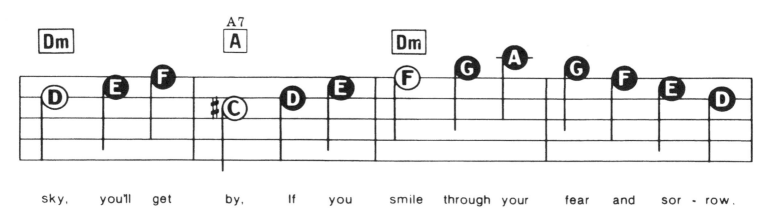

sky, you'll get by, If you smile through your fear and sor - row.

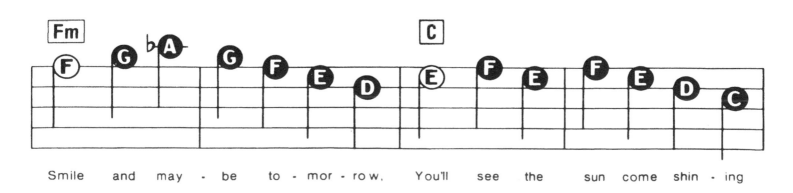

Smile and may - be to - mor - row, You'll see the sun come shin - ing

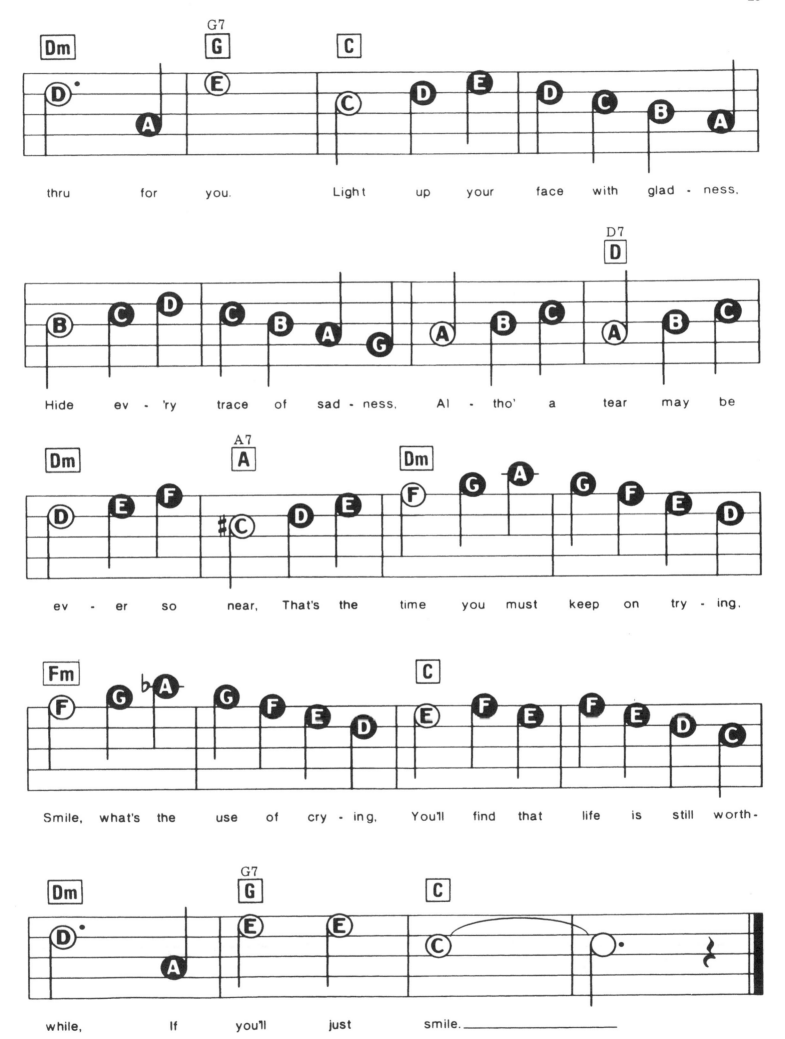

That Old Feeling

Registration 4
Rhythm: Swing or Big Band

Words and Music by Lew Brown
and Sammy Fain

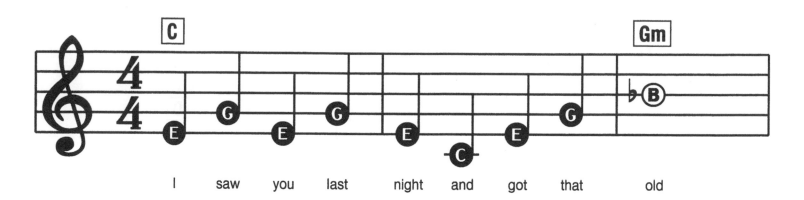

I saw you last night and got that old

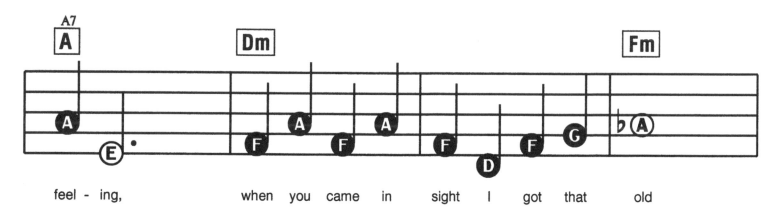

feel - ing, when you came in sight I got that old

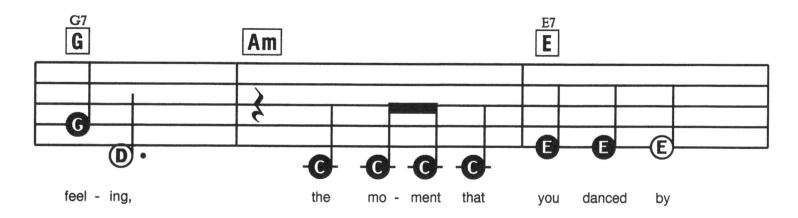

feel - ing, the mo - ment that you danced by

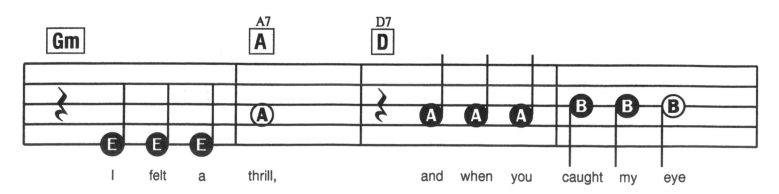

I felt a thrill, and when you caught my eye

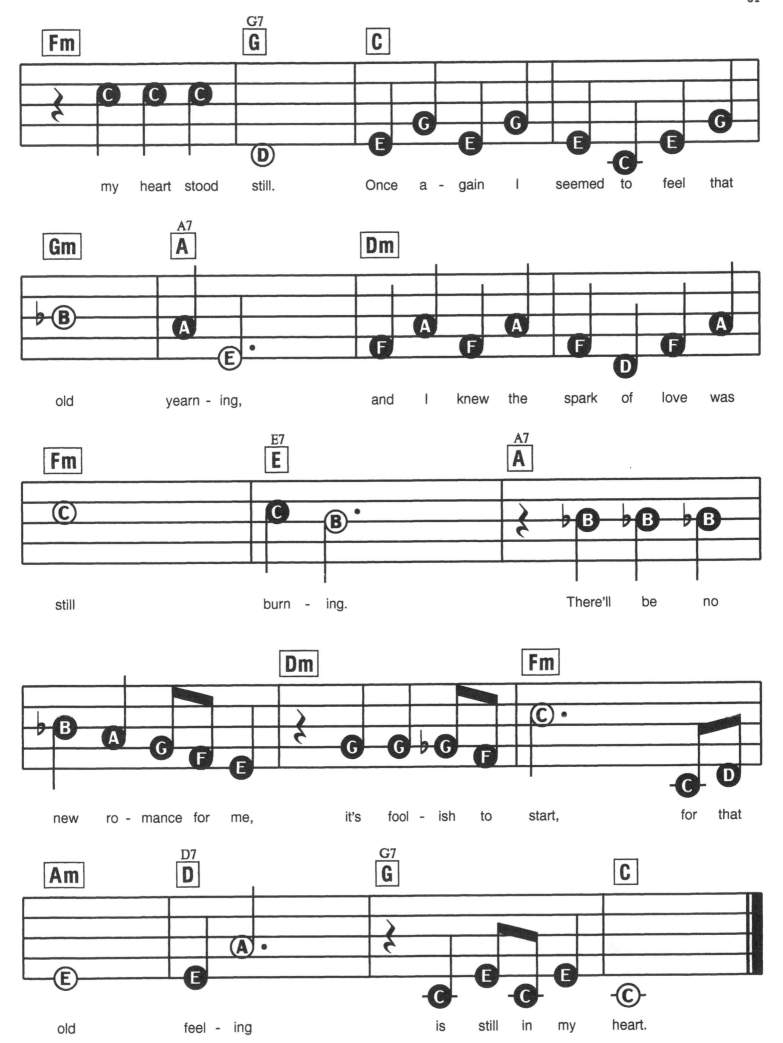

These Foolish Things
(Remind Me of You)

Registration 9
Rhythm: Fox Trot

Words by Holt Marvell
Music by Jack Strachey

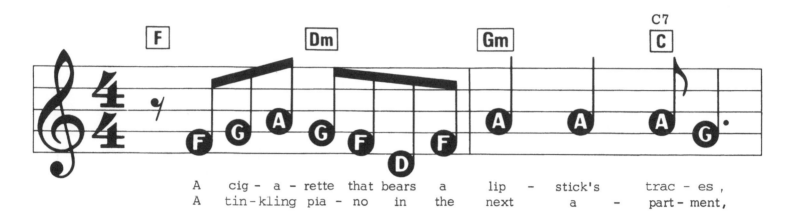

A cig - a - rette that bears a lip - stick's trac - es,
A tin - kling pia - no in the next a - part - ment,

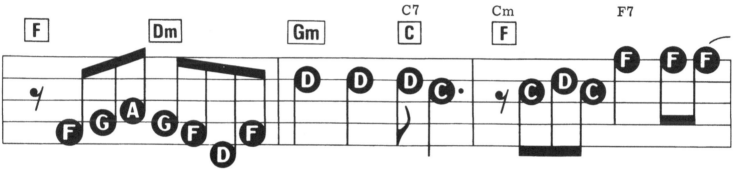

An air - line tick - et to ro - man - tic plac - es,
Those stum - bling words that told you what my heart meant,
And still my heart has wings.
A fair - ground's paint - ed swings,

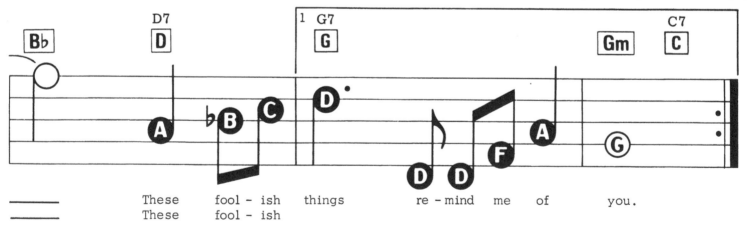

These fool - ish things re - mind me of you.
These fool - ish

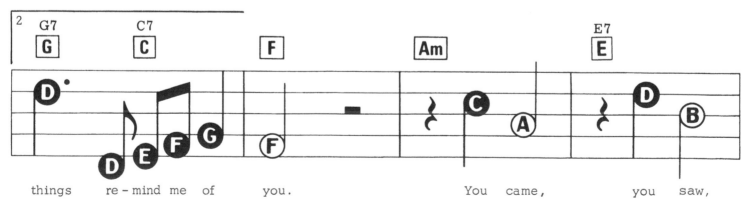

things re - mind me of you.
You came, you saw,

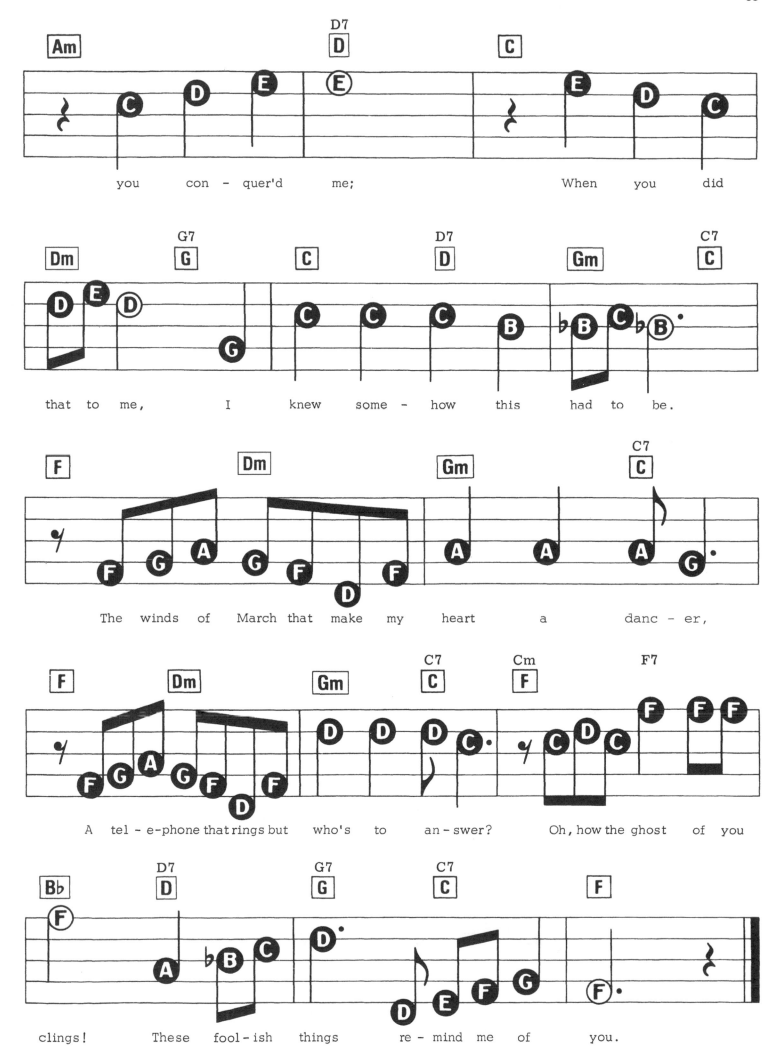

Till There Was You
from Meredith Willson's THE MUSIC MAN

Registration 2
Rhythm: Ballad

By Meredith Willson

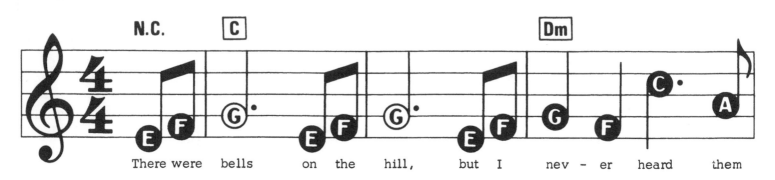

There were bells on the hill, but I nev-er heard them

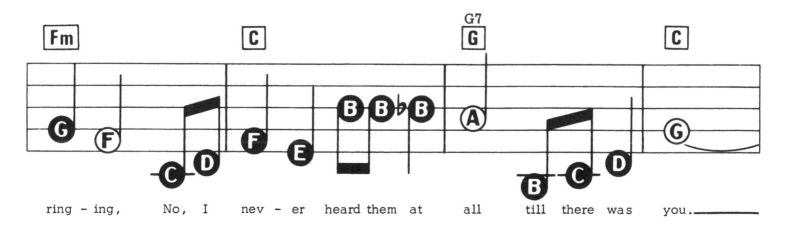

ring-ing, No, I nev-er heard them at all till there was you._____

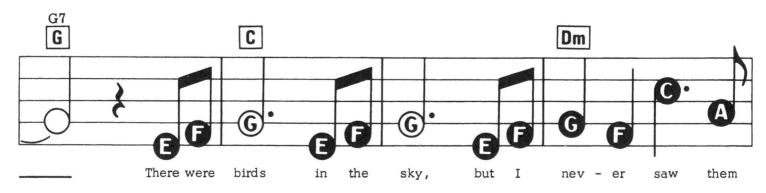

_____ There were birds in the sky, but I nev-er saw them

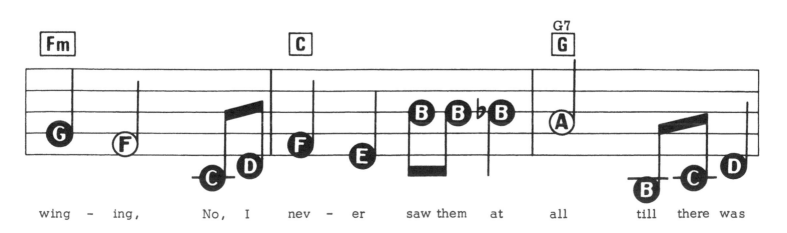

wing-ing, No, I nev-er saw them at all till there was

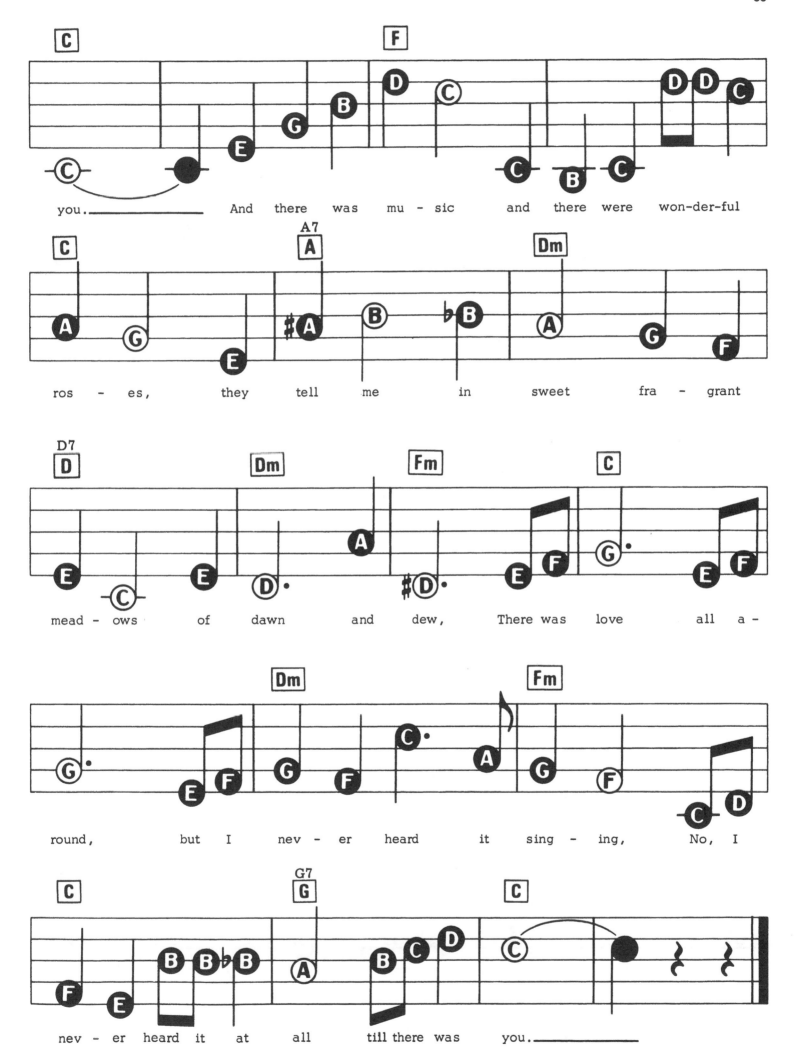

Time After Time
from the Metro-Goldwyn-Mayer Picture IT HAPPENED IN BROOKLYN

Registration 5
Rhythm: Fox Trot or Ballad

Words by Sammy Cahn
Music by Jule Styne

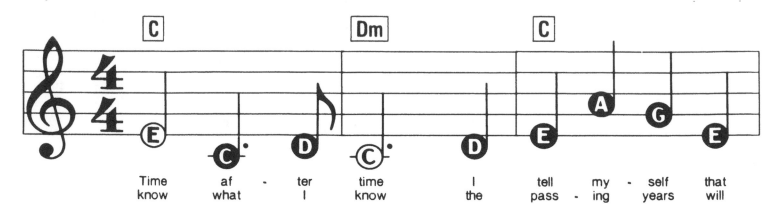

Time af - ter time I
know what I know the

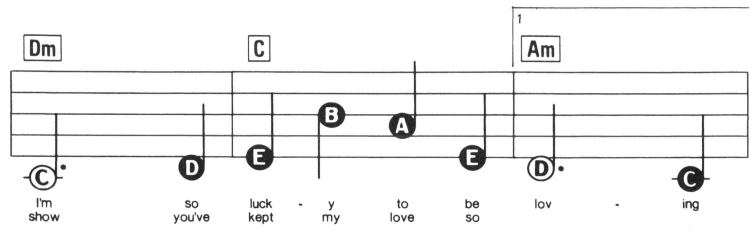

I'm so luck - y to be lov - ing
show you've kept my love so

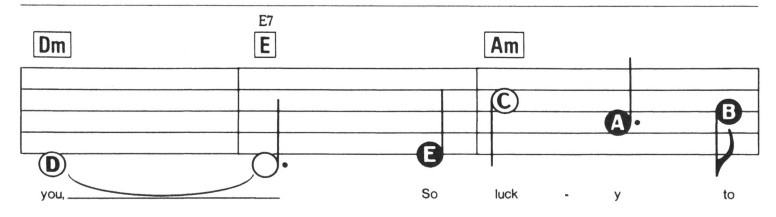

you, _____ So luck - y to

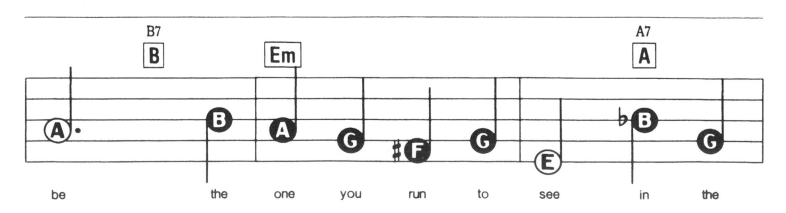

be the one you run to see in the

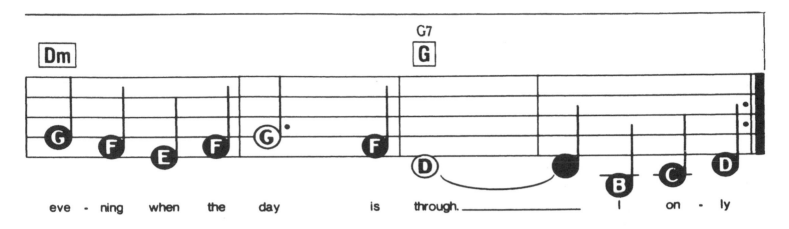

eve - ning when the day is through. _____ I on - ly

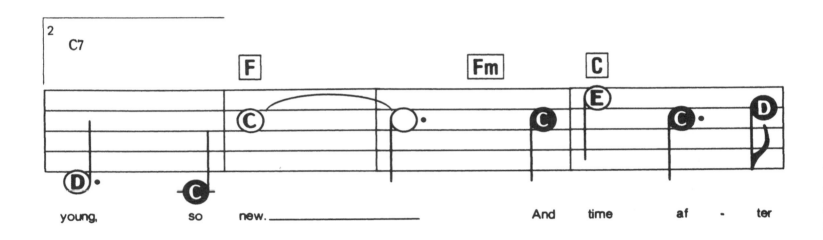

young, so new. _____ And time af - ter

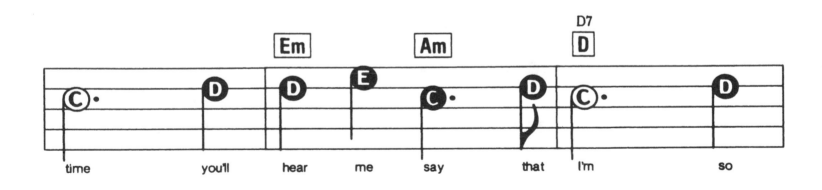

time you'll hear me say that I'm so

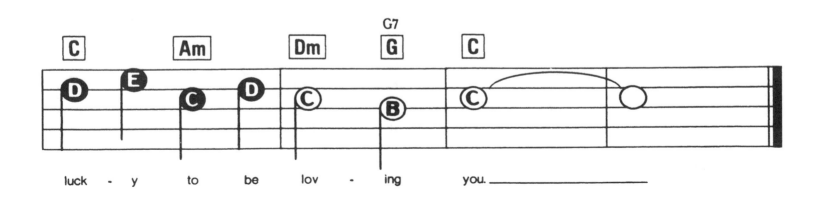

luck - y to be lov - ing you. _____

The Very Thought of You

Registration 8
Rhythm: Ballad or Fox Trot

Words and Music by
Ray Noble

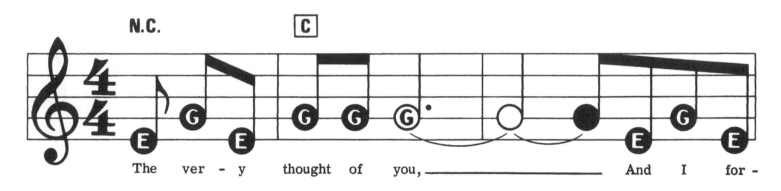

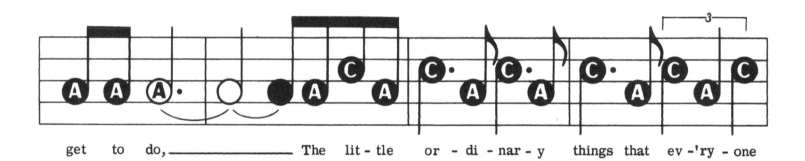

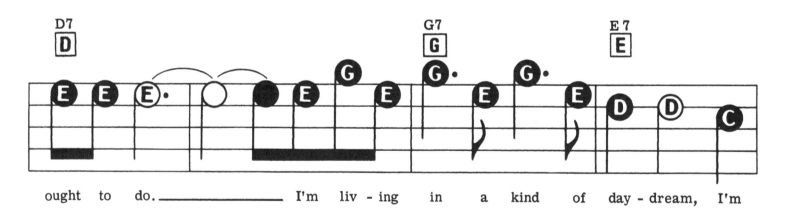

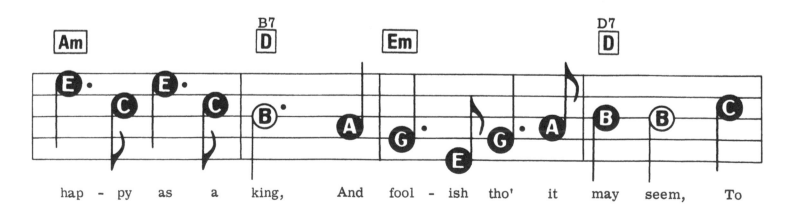

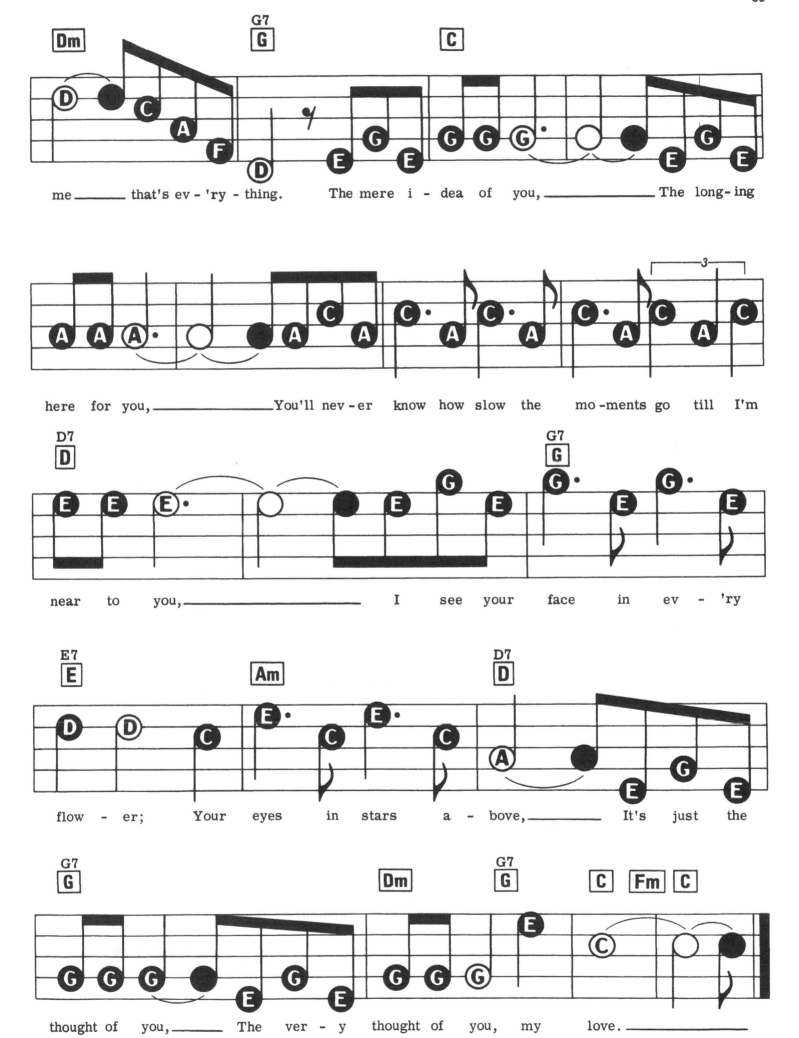

The Way You Look Tonight
from SWING TIME

Registration 3
Rhythm: Fox Trot or Ballad

Words by Dorothy Fields
Music by Jerome Kern

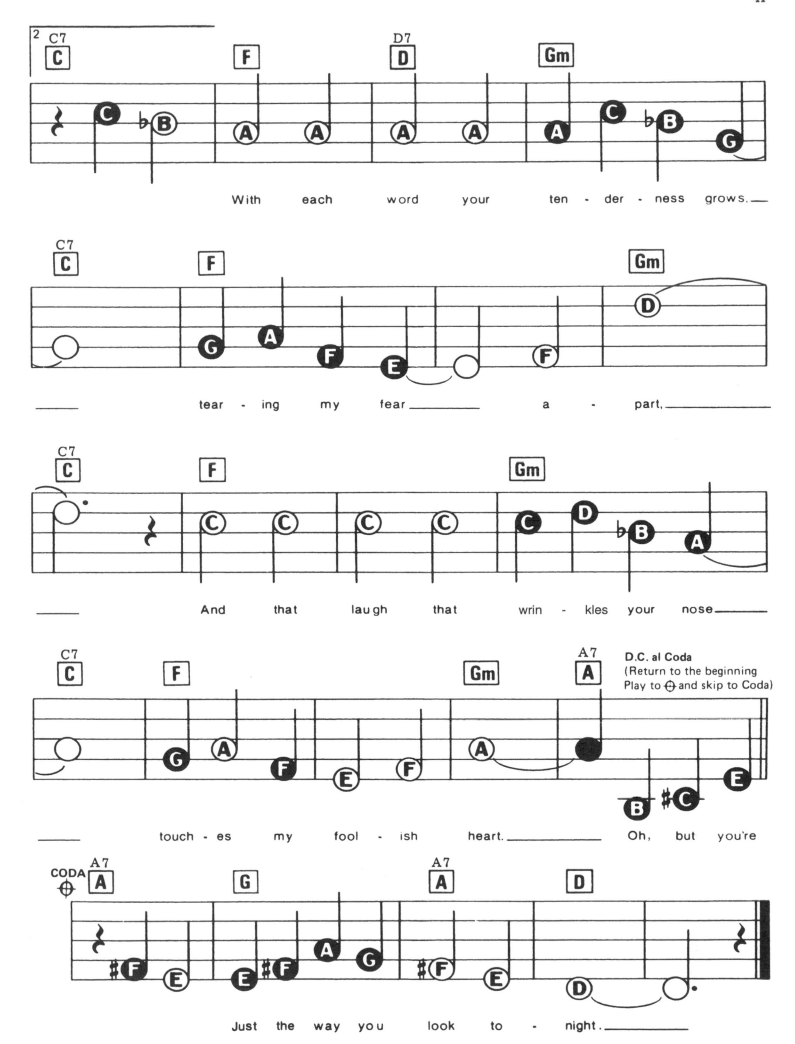

What a Wonderful World

Registration 2
Rhythm: Ballad

Words and Music by George David Weiss
and Bob Thiele

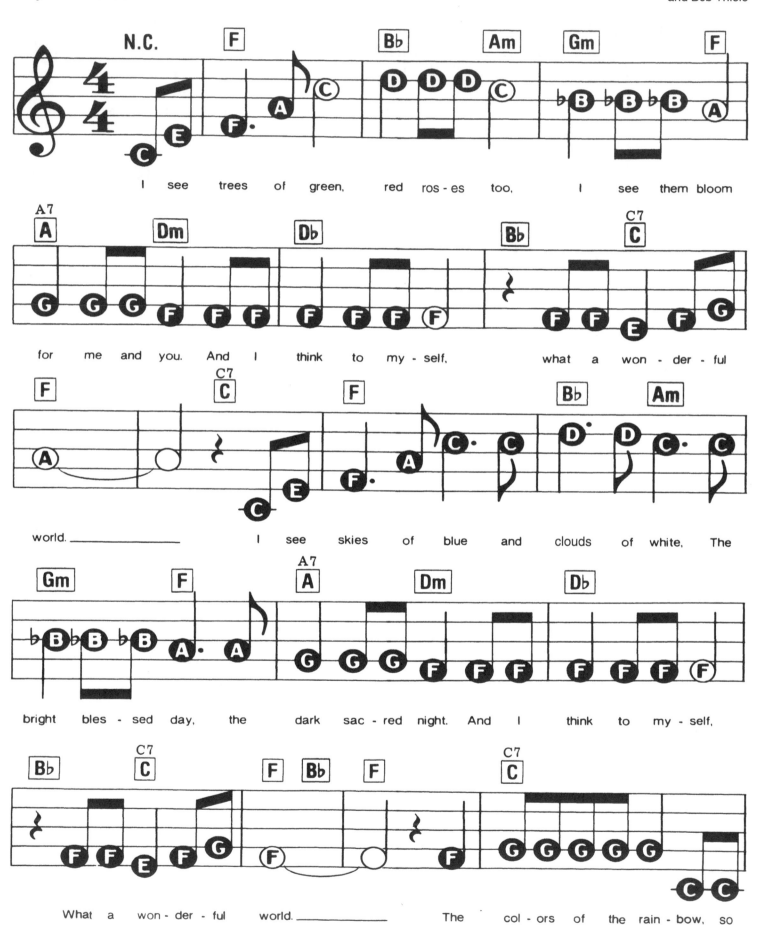

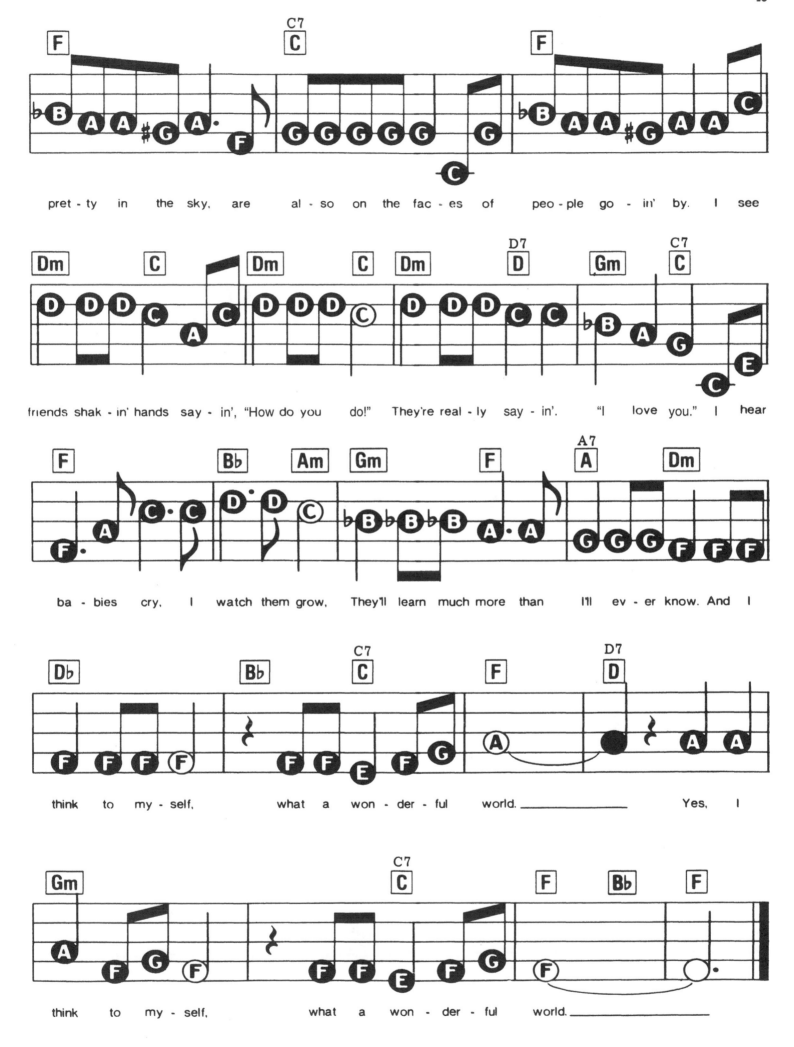

pret - ty in the sky, are al - so on the fac - es of peo - ple go - in' by. I see

friends shak - in' hands say - in', "How do you do!" They're real - ly say - in'. "I love you." I hear

ba - bies cry, I watch them grow, They'll learn much more than I'll ev - er know. And I

think to my - self, what a won - der - ful world. _____ Yes, I

think to my - self, what a won - der - ful world. _____

Where or When
from BABES IN ARMS

Registration 7
Rhythm: Fox Trot or Ballad

Words by Lorenz Hart
Music by Richard Rodgers

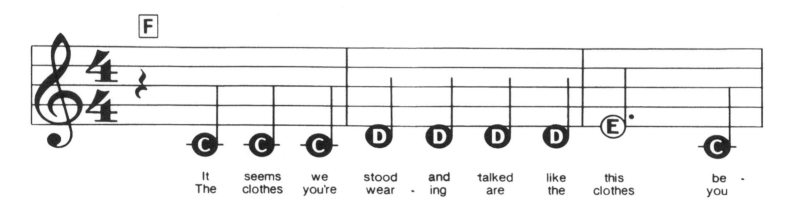

It seems we stood and talked like this be
The clothes you're wear-ing are the clothes you

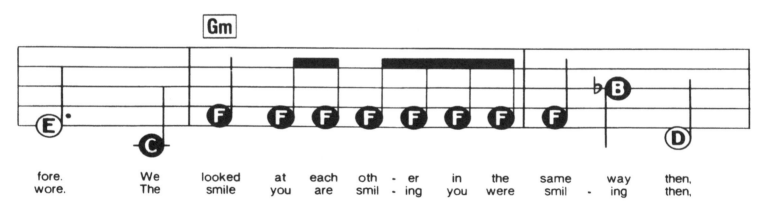

fore. We looked at each oth-er in the same way then,
wore. The smile you are smil-ing you were smil-ing then,

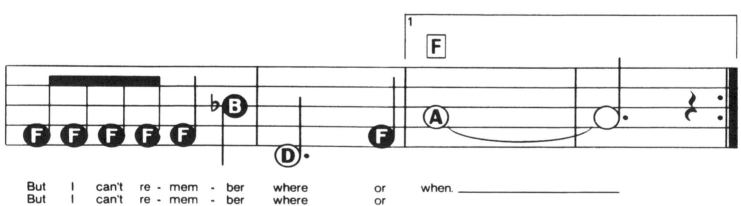

But I can't re-mem-ber where or when. _____
But I can't re-mem-ber where or

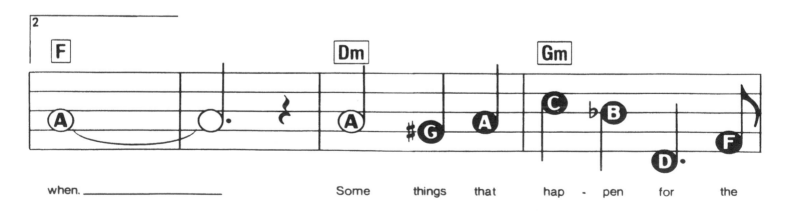

when. _____ Some things that hap-pen for the

45

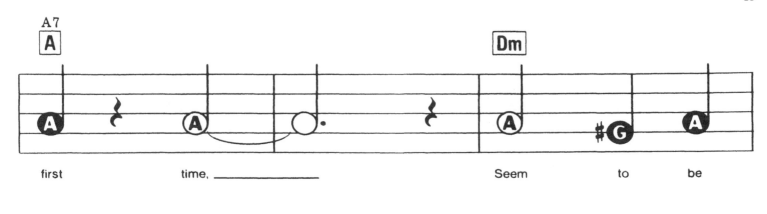

first time, _____ Seem to be

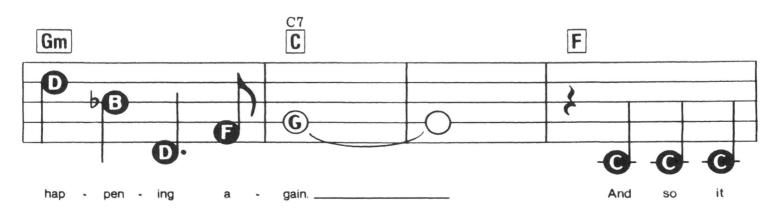

hap - pen - ing a - gain. _____ And so it

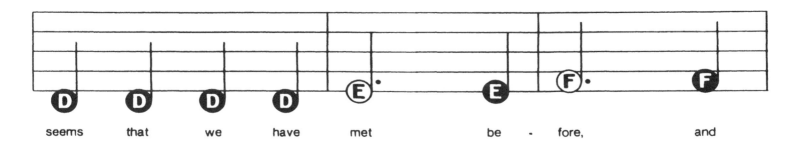

seems that we have met be - fore, and

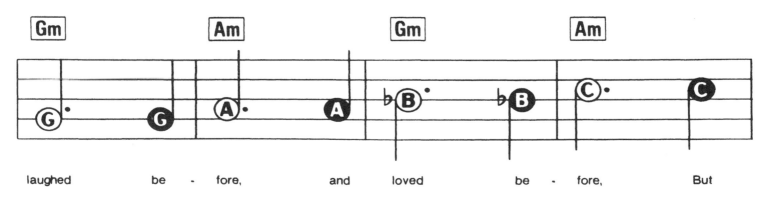

laughed be - fore, and loved be - fore, But

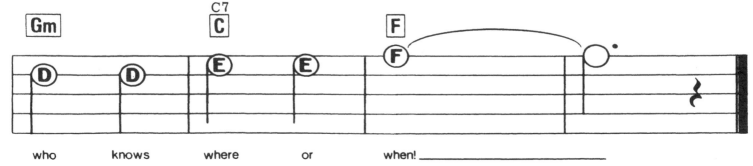

who knows where or when! _____

Registration Guide

- Match the Registration number on the song to the corresponding numbered category below. Select and activate an instrumental sound available on your instrument.

- Choose an automatic rhythm appropriate to the mood and style of the song. (Consult your Owner's Guide for proper operation of automatic rhythm features.)

- Adjust the tempo and volume controls to comfortable settings.

Registration

1	Mellow	Flutes, Clarinet, Oboe, Flugel Horn, Trombone, French Horn, Organ Flutes
2	Ensemble	Brass Section, Sax Section, Wind Ensemble, Full Organ, Theater Organ
3	Strings	Violin, Viola, Cello, Fiddle, String Ensemble, Pizzicato, Organ Strings
4	Guitars	Acoustic/Electric Guitars, Banjo, Mandolin, Dulcimer, Ukulele, Hawaiian Guitar
5	Mallets	Vibraphone, Marimba, Xylophone, Steel Drums, Bells, Celesta, Chimes
6	Liturgical	Pipe Organ, Hand Bells, Vocal Ensemble, Choir, Organ Flutes
7	Bright	Saxophones, Trumpet, Mute Trumpet, Synth Leads, Jazz/Gospel Organs
8	Piano	Piano, Electric Piano, Honky Tonk Piano, Harpsichord, Clavi
9	Novelty	Melodic Percussion, Wah Trumpet, Synth, Whistle, Kazoo, Perc. Organ
10	Bellows	Accordion, French Accordion, Mussette, Harmonica, Pump Organ, Bagpipes